READ ALOUD

FOLK TALES

The Terrified Ghost

............and other Stories

Retold by

VANEETA VAID

READ ALOUD

FOLK TALES

The Terrified Ghost

............and other Stories

Nita Mehta Publications
Enriching Young Minds

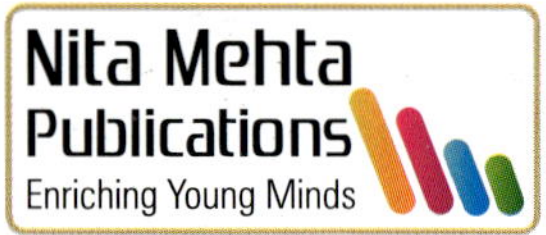

Nita Mehta Publications

Corporate Office
3A/3, Asaf Ali Road, New Delhi 110 002
Phone: +91 11 2325 2948, 2325 0091
Telefax: +91 11 2325 0091
E-mail: nitamehta@nitamehta.com
Website: www.nitamehta.com

ISBN 978-81-7676-118-5

First Print 2013

Printed in India at Infinity Advertising Services (P) Ltd, New Delhi

Editorial and Marketing office
E-159, Greater Kailash II, New Delhi 110 048

Typesetting by National Information Technology Academy
3A/3, Asaf Ali Road, New Delhi 110 002

Nita Mehta Books
Distributors & Publishers

Distributed by :
NITA MEHTA BOOKS
3A/3, Asaf Ali Road, New Delhi - 02

Distribution Centre :
D16/1, Okhla Industrial Area, Phase-I,
New Delhi - 110020
Tel.: 26813199, 26813200
E-mail: nitamehta.mehta@gmail.com

Contributing Writers:
Subhash Mehta
Tanya Mehta

Editorial & Proofreading:
Rajesh
Ramesh

Price: Rs. 145/-

CONTENTS

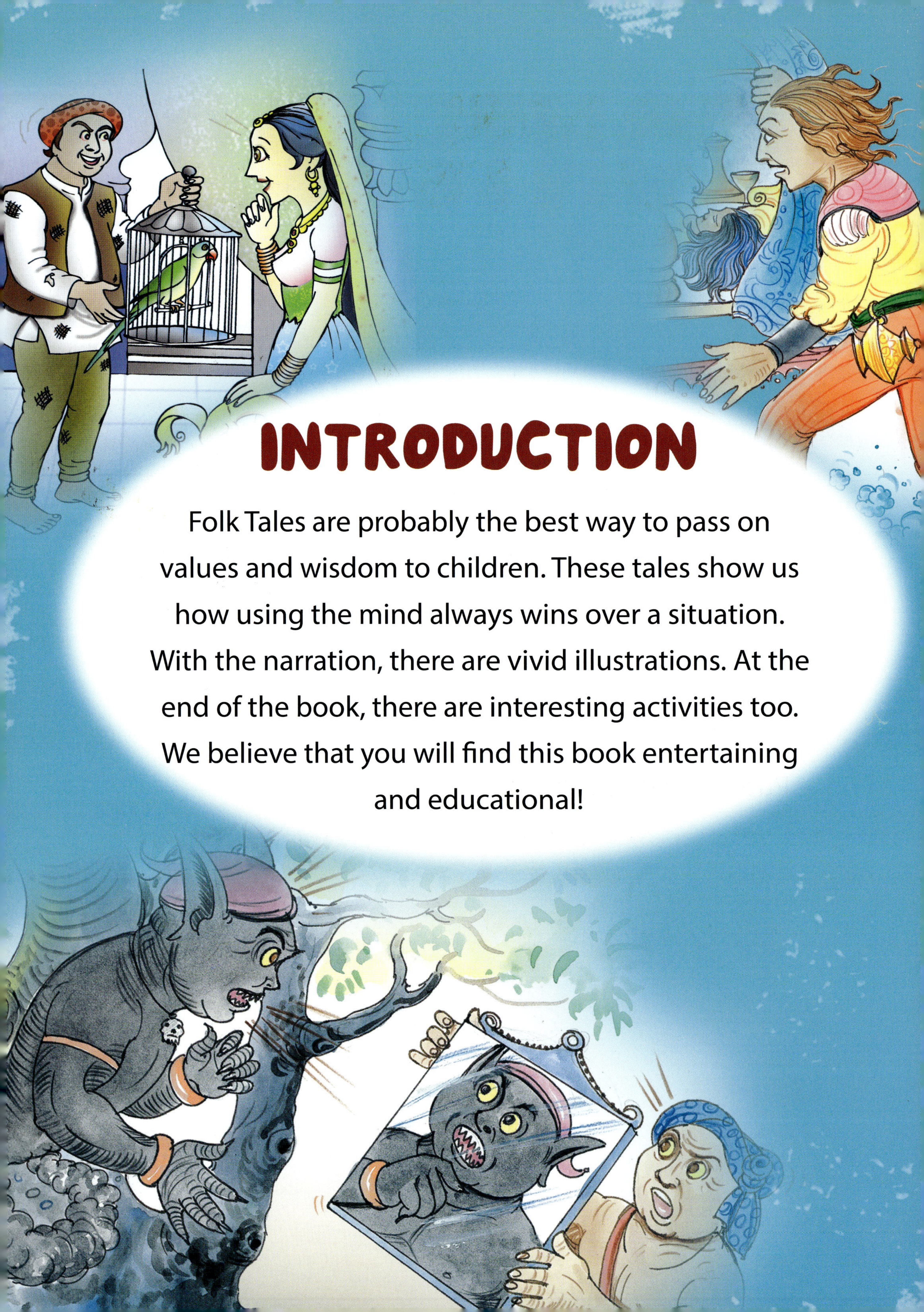

INTRODUCTION

Folk Tales are probably the best way to pass on values and wisdom to children. These tales show us how using the mind always wins over a situation. With the narration, there are vivid illustrations. At the end of the book, there are interesting activities too. We believe that you will find this book entertaining and educational!

THE MAGIC SHOES

Prince Putraka was attacked by armed men.

He was very sad to know that the men had been sent by his own relatives.

They wanted him dead, so they could take away his kingdom.

Putraka managed to save himself by bribing the men, by giving them his crown and jewels.

Putraka quickly escaped.

Putraka ran and reached the forest.

In the forest, two demons were fighting.

Next to them, lay a pair of shoes, a stick and a cooking pot.

"Why are you two fighting?" asked Putraka.

"For those. These are no ordinary things! They are magical. Draw imaginary drawings in the air and the stick makes them real! The pot cooks any meal on its own! The shoes make you fly!" said the two demons.

Putraka decided he wanted these things for himself.

"I shall help you settle who should get these three things!" said Putraka.

The demons immediately stopped fighting.

"You should have a race. Whosoever wins the race gets the things."

The demons raced off. Putraka seizing his opportunity, grabbed the pot, the stick and the shoes and ran off in another direction.

When he was at a safe distance, he wore the shoes. "WHEEEEEE!" Putraka started flying!

He flew all over.

Finally Putraka landed.

"Let me find a place to stay," said he.

An old lady allowed Putraka to stay in her hut with her. She also told Putraka about the beautiful princess, called Patali. Patali was captured in a palace tower by her father, the king of the lands.

Putraka decided to rescue the princess. With the help of the shoes, he flew into the palace.

The princess fell in love with Putraka the moment she set eyes on him. They quickly left the tower.

Putraka flew to a great distance before he landed.

At once, Putraka pulled out the magic pot and said, “Give us food!” Delicious food appeared. Seeing the power of the shoes and the pot, Patali asked, “What is that stick for?”

“Whatever I draw with it becomes real,” answered Putraka.

“Then draw a city for us to live. Also draw an army to defeat my father! I hear him coming! My father is here,” Patali cried. This is what Putraka did! He quickly sketched a city and an army!

Putraka's army soon defeated his father-in-law's army. Putraka and Patali lived happily ever after.

A PIG'S LIFE

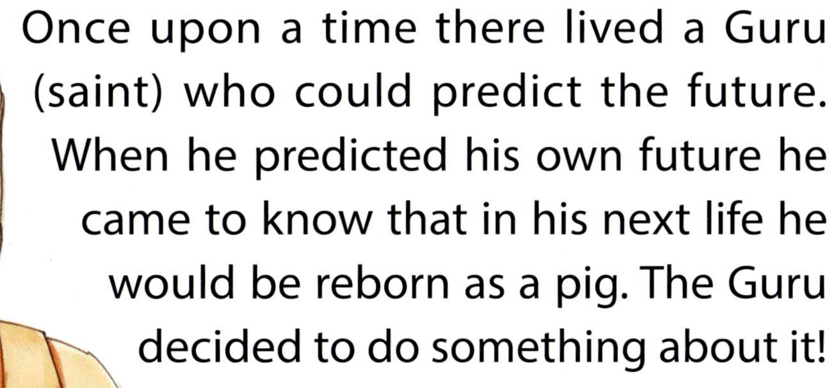

Once upon a time there lived a Guru (saint) who could predict the future. When he predicted his own future he came to know that in his next life he would be reborn as a pig. The Guru decided to do something about it!

He called his student and said,

"Son, after I die I shall be reborn as a pig. See the tilak (vermillion dot) on my forehead. In our farm yard when the mother pig has her piglets, the piglet with this mark will be me! After living like a guru, I hate to live a pig's life. As soon as you identify the mark, please kill me."

The student agreed to follow his guru's instructions.

Very soon, the guru died. After a few months, the student saw that the mother pig in the farm yard had babies. *In her brood, there was a piglet with the mark*!

“That is my Guru!” the student exclaimed.

He quickly brought a knife to kill the piglet with the mark.

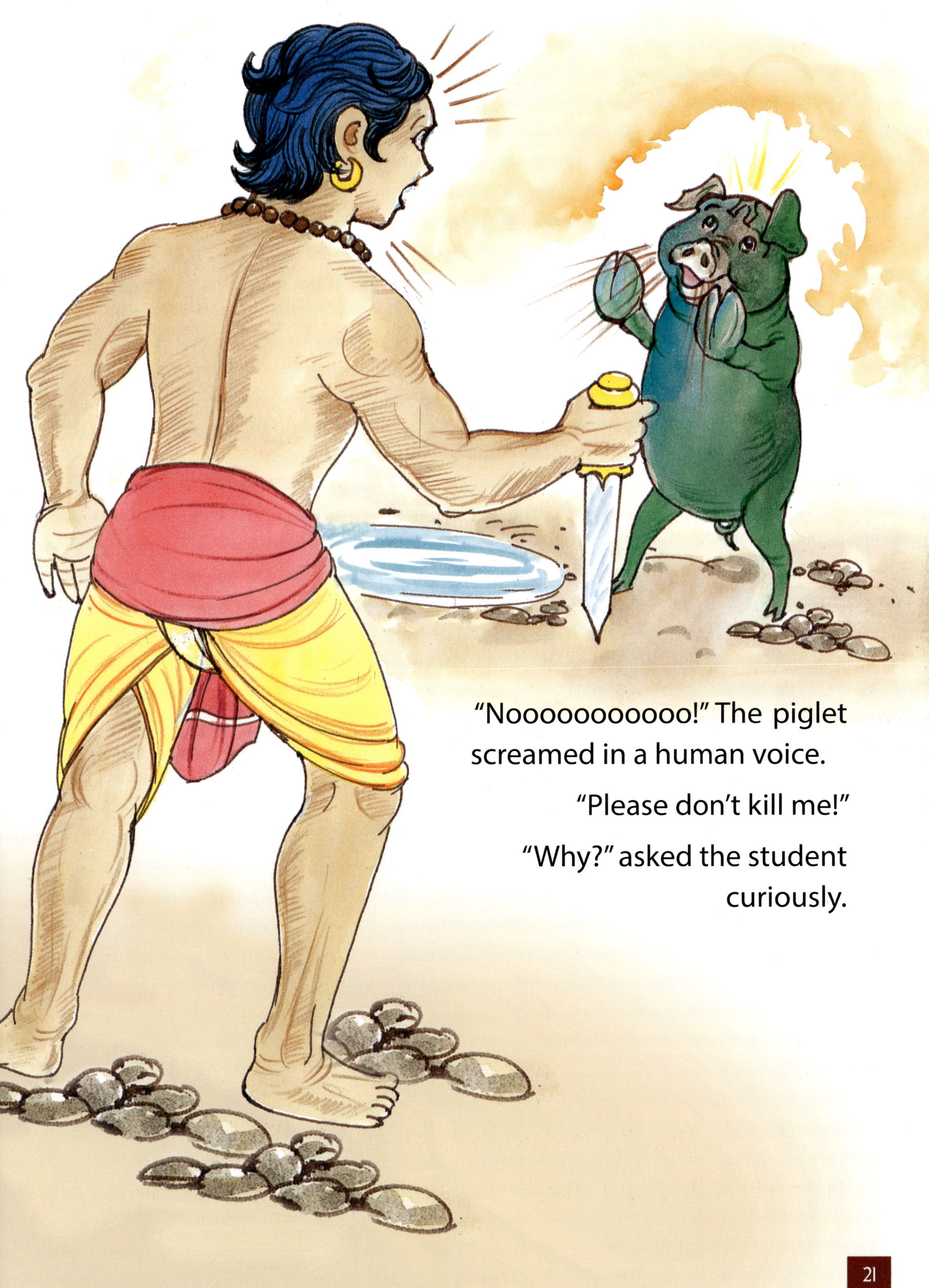

"Noooooooooooo!" The piglet screamed in a human voice.

"Please don't kill me!"

"Why?" asked the student curiously.

"Now that I'm here, I like it. This mud is comfortable. I nestle close to my loving mother who feeds me delicious milk. Please let me be!"

The student agreed. Later, the student brought the piglet home and raised it with loving care.

THE TERRIFIED GHOST

A barber sat under a tree where a ghost lived. The ghost seeing the barber lunged out from the tree and howled. He wanted to scare the barber, you see. The barber refused to be scared!

The ghost was so shocked.

"Why are you not scared?" asked the ghost.

The barber was a clever man. He decided to fool the ghost.

"I trap ghosts in my bag! See!" The barber held up his barber's mirror. The ghost saw his own reflection! But he did not realize that! The ghost actually believed that the barber had trapped a ghost.

"Oh no, please don't trap me!" cried the terrified ghost.

"I can leave you on one condition," said the barber.

"(sob) I will do anything for you, anything!" wailed the ghost.

"Ghosts have powers of invisibility. Go to the treasury and get me a thousand coins of gold," ordered the barber.

The ghost became invisible. He entered the treasury to lift off one thousand gold coins!

“Good,” said the Barber. “Now with your powers, build me a granary near my house and fill it up!”

That is exactly what the ghost did. He even told all the other ghosts that a ghost trapper was looking for them! They curiously went to the barber!

The barber scared away all the ghosts with his mirror! The rich barber happily lived with his wife ever after.

THE LIES HE TOLD...

Kewal was a liar. One day, he met a stranger at the village square. He lied to him, too. "I am a rich man!" boasted Kewal untruthfully.

He pointed to a rich lady, distributing food to the poor, and lied, "My wife has sent her maid here to feed the poor. You sit and eat too."

Meanwhile the rich lady, approached the stranger and Kewal. She served them food also.

"Look, how generous my wife is! She keeps the maid dressed so well..." Kewal commented .

"You are wondering why I am wearing these rags, eh?" The stranger gulped, too polite to agree. Kewal lied again, "You see, my wife has taken an oath, that we will wear rags for forty days. Too much of money can make others jealous! We pray day and night for good will to all!" Kewal lied.

"Do you want me to pray for you too?" Kewal asked the stranger. The stranger completely fooled by Kewal's lies, nodded. "Then give me some money for the prayers since one should pray with one's own money!"

The stranger took out some money and handed it to Kewal. "I will leave now. I see my security men waiting for me down the street!" announced Kewal.

Impressed, the stranger thought that Kewal was a great man! He never realized that Kewal was lying!

Down the road were the landlord's henchmen who had come looking for Kewal!

As soon as the henchmen saw Kewal, they began to beat him!

The landlord was very angry!! After all, who can blame him?

Kewal had sold his wife, a parrot, for a hefty sum! He had said it could sing in ten different languages!

It was Kewal's bad luck that the village school teacher, on seeing the 'singing' parrot, said it was a wild one. It had been trapped from the nearby forest. The parrot therefore could never talk; let alone sing!

The henchmen hesitated however, when Kewal hung his head and started crying softly. He told the landlord's men that he had fooled the lady because he needed money to pay for his dying wife's medical bills.

"Come, come, I will show her to you!" said he. Reaching home, a terrible wail came from his shack. "Please, don't go in, she hates to be seen like this," said Kewal sobbing. Convinced, they patted Kewal's shoulder in sympathy and left.

Now, how were they to know that it was not Kewal's wife wailing, but the neighbour's sick dog. The dog was tied up in his shack as Kewal had promised his neighbour, a miracle drug for the ill dog.

THE TALKING CAVE

One day, Toothy, a ferocious lion fell down a grassy hill!

“Bump-bump-thump!” he fell near a cave entrance.

“I am hungry! I will go into the cave and lie low! All animals take shelter in caves. Let the animal enter and I shall pounce and eat it,” the lion happily decided.

He entered the cave and lay down quietly.

Now, Toothy did not know that in this particular cave lived Chackal, the jackal.

When Chackal returned in the evening to the cave, he had a bad feeling.

He also noticed lion pug marks near the cave!

'Is there a lion inside?' he wondered.

Chackal decided against going into the cave, before he was very sure that there was no lion inside!

Clearing his throat, he loudly called.

"Hello cave! How are you today? Please, may I enter?"

The lion lay still, as quiet as a mouse.

Again, Chackal the jackal, raised his voice higher and asked, "Cave, dear cave, give me permission to enter."

The lion remained still, holding his breath.

"Oh, my dear cave, talk to me. Why are you not talking? Is there something wrong? Tell me?" the jackal cried.

Toothy thought, 'The cave is quiet. It is warning the jackal! I had better do something!'

Toothy decided to imitate a talking cave.

But lions can only roar! So, instead of using proper words, Toothy roared! He thought that sounded like a talking cave you see! He went,

"ROARRRRRR!"

The roar echoed through the forest. Chackal the jackal ran away as fast as he could!

Clever of you, Chackal the jackal! As for you, Toothy the lion; how in the world did you get the idea that caves can talk?

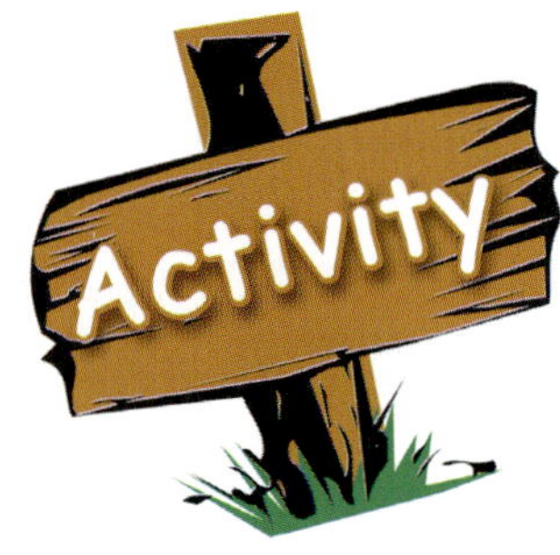

EVERY PICTURE HAS A NUMBER IN THE BOX BELOW. CHECK AND ADD THE NUMBERS.

CLUE BOX

5	8	2	7	9	3

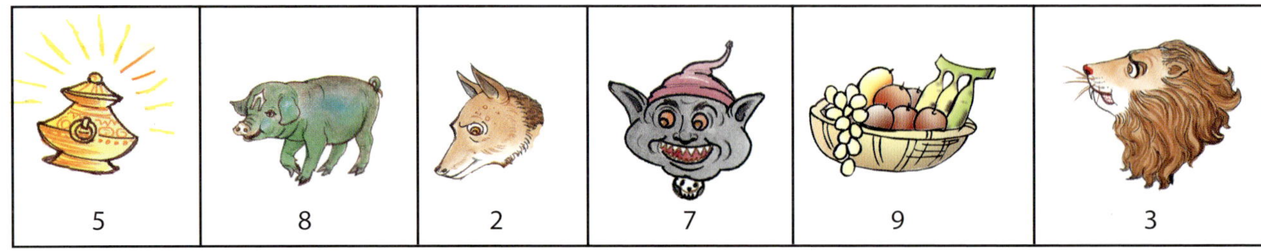

Example

(a) 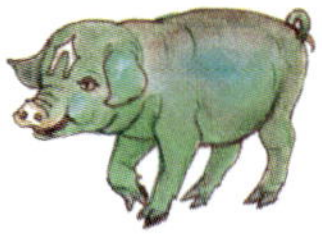 + 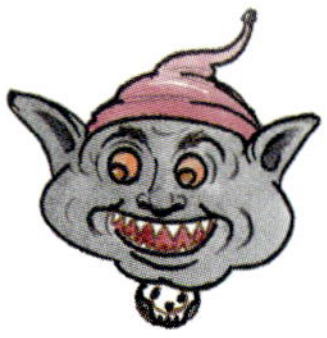 = **15**

(b) 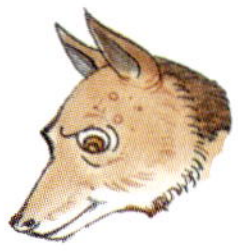 + 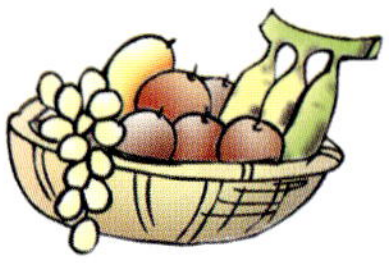 = ________

(c) 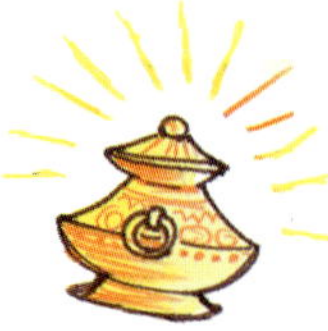 + 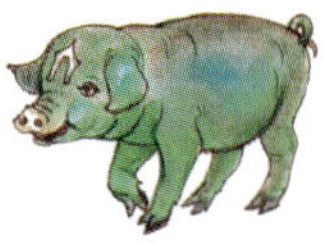 = ________

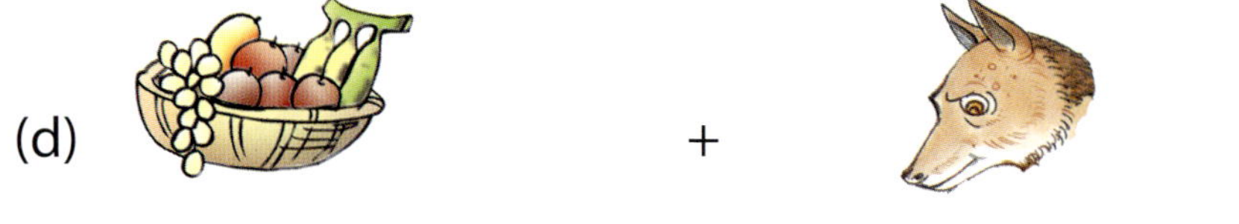

(d) + = ________

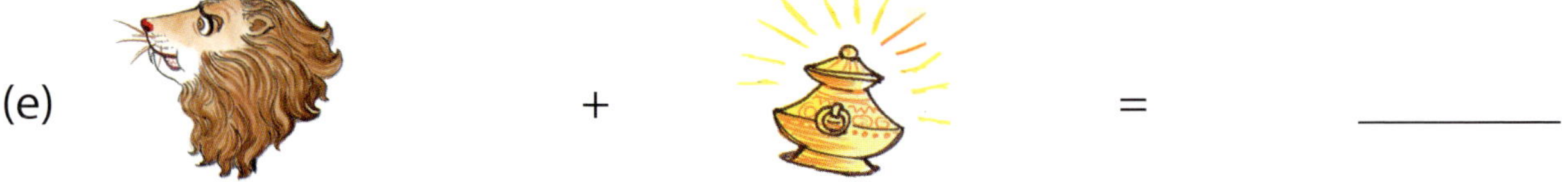

(e) + = ________

Answers: (b) 11, (c) 13, (d) 11, (e) 8

Activity
HELP THE PIGLET
FIND HIS MOTHER

FILL IN THE MISSING LETTERS TO COMPLETE THE WORDS TAKEN FROM THE STORIES.

P_INC_

(a)

CA_E

(b)

BA_ _ER

(c)

G_O_T

(d)

ST_DEN_

(e)

PA_ _OT

(f)

Answers : (a) PRINCE, (b) CAVE, (c) BARBER, (d) GHOST, (e) STUDENT, (f) PARROT